Le...

To the untutored, creative a... forms of thought — the fir... the second on rational and conscious processes; the first undirectable and unteachable, the second directable and teachable. There is some, but very little, truth in this view. The truth in it is that there is no known way to generate creative geniuses, or to get students to produce novel, ground-breaking ideas. There are manifestations of creativity that we do not fully understand. The same is true of forms of criticality. Yet there are ways to teach simultaneously for both creative and critical thinking. To do so requires that we focus on these terms in practical, everyday contexts, that we keep their central meanings in mind, that we seek insight into how they overlap and interact with one another. When we understand critical and creative thought truly and deeply, we recognize them as inseparable, integrated, and unitary.

We believe that creative thinking, especially, must be demystified and brought down to earth. For this reason, we deal with it in this guide not only in terms of its highest manifestation (in the work of geniuses), but also in its most humble manifestations (in everyday perception and thought).

In learning new concepts, in making sense of our experience, in apprehending a new subject field or language, in reading, writing, speaking, and listening, our minds engage in full-fledged (though commonplace) creative acts. To understand how and why this is so, we need not appeal to the esoteric, the recondite, or the arcane.

To live productively, we need to internalize and use intellectual standards to assess our thinking (criticality). We also need to generate — through creative acts of the mind — the products to be assessed. That minds create meanings is not in doubt; whether they create meanings that are useful, insightful, or profound is. Imagination and reason are an inseparable team. They function best in tandem, like the right and left legs in walking or running. Studying either one separately only ensures that both remain mysterious and puzzling, or, just as unfortunate, are reduced to stereotype and caricature.

Richard Paul
Center for Critical Thinking

Linda Elder
Foundation for Critical Thinking

Contents

Part I: The Very Idea of Critical and Creative Thinking

Part II: Critical/Creative Thinking and the Foundations of Meaningfulness

PART I
The Very Idea of
Critical and Creative Thinking

The Inseparability of Critical and Creative Thought

The critical and creative functions of the mind are so interwoven that neither can be separated from the other without an essential loss to both.
— *Anonymous*

Criticality assesses; creativity originates.

For several reasons the relationship between criticality and creativity is commonly misunderstood. One reason is cultural, resulting largely from the mass media's portrayal of creative and critical persons. The media frequently represent the creative person as a cousin to the nutty professor, highly imaginative, spontaneous, emotional, a source of off-beat ideas, but often out of touch with everyday reality. The critical person, in turn, is wrongly represented as given to fault-finding, as skeptical, negative, captious, severe, and hypercritical; as focused on trivial faults, either unduly exacting or perversely hard to please; lacking in spontaneity, imagination, and emotion.

These cultural stereotypes are not validated by precise use of the words critical and creative. For example, in *Webster's Dictionary of Synonyms*, the word "critical,"

> when applied to persons who judge and to their judgments, not only may, but in very precise use does, imply an effort to see a thing clearly and truly so that not only the good in it may be distinguished from the bad and the perfect from the imperfect, but also that it as a whole may be fairly judged and valued.

In *Webster's New World Dictionary*, the word "creative" has three interrelated meanings:

> 1) creating or able to create, 2) having or showing imagination and artistic or intellectual inventiveness (creative writing), and 3) stimulating the imagination and inventive powers.

Accordingly, ***critical*** and ***creative*** thought are both achievements of thought. Creativity masters a process of making or producing, criticality a process of assessing or judging. The very definition of the word "creative" implies a critical component (e.g., "having or showing imagination and artistic or intellectual inventiveness"). When engaged in high-quality thought, the mind must simultaneously produce and assess, both generate and judge the products it fabricates. In short, sound thinking requires both imagination and intellectual standards.

Throughout this guide we elaborate on the essential idea that intellectual discipline and rigor are at home with originality and productivity, and also that these supposed poles of thinking (critical and creative thought) are inseparable aspects of excellence of thought. Whether we are dealing with the most mundane intellectual acts of the mind or those of the most imaginative artist or thinker, the creative and the critical are interwoven. It is the nature of the mind to create thoughts, though the quality of that creation varies enormously from person to person, as well as from thought to thought. Achieving quality requires standards of quality — and hence, criticality.

In this guide, then, we explore the interdependence of criticality and creativity, exemplifying this interdependence at the most complex level of thought (that of genius) as well as the simplest level of thought (that of making sense of ordinary objects in everyday experience).

We also explore a corollary theme: that all creation of meaning tends toward systems of meanings rather than existing in the mind as unconnected atomic particles. This is integral to the nature of thought itself. The construction of any meaning assumes other meanings and implies yet further meanings (which in turn imply still further meanings). When attempting to understand any meaning, humans naturally seek to place it in a cluster of meanings, however partial their understanding might be. When they attempt to understand an idea as a thing unto itself, it doesn't take root in the mind. It doesn't connect to the systems of meanings within the mind. In short, for humans to think well, we must think within systems. We must create systems of meaning and assess our creations for accuracy, relevance, and adequacy. More on this point later.

Let's begin with some fundamentals. First, ***all thinking is not of the same quality***. High-quality thinking is thinking that does the job set for it. It is thinking that accomplishes the purposes of thinking. If thinking lacks a purpose — if it is aimless — it may chance upon something of value to the thinker. But more often it will simply wander into an endless stream of unanalyzed associations from one's unanalyzed past: "Hotdogs remind me of

ballgames, ballgames remind me of Chicago, Chicago of my old neighborhood, my old neighborhood of my grandmother, of her pies, of having to eat what I didn't like, which reminds me…which reminds me…which reminds me…"
Few people need training in aimless thinking such as this, or in daydreaming or fantasizing. For the most part, we are naturals at aimless thinking. We are inherently proficient at daydreaming and fantasizing.

However, we often have trouble in purposeful thinking, especially purposeful thinking that requires posing problems and reasoning through intricacies. Purposeful thinking requires both critical and creative thinking. Both are intimately connected to figuring things out. There is a natural marriage between them. Indeed, all truly excellent thinking combines these two dimensions. Whenever our thinking excels, it excels because we succeed in designing or engendering, fashioning or originating, creating or producing results and outcomes appropriate to our ends in thinking. It has, in a word, a creative dimension.

To achieve any challenging end, though, we also must have criteria: gauges, measures, models, principles, standards, or tests to use in judging whether we are approaching that end. What's more, we must apply our criteria in a way that is discerning, discriminating, exacting, and judicious. We must continually monitor and assess how our thinking is going, whether it is on the right track, whether it is sufficiently clear, accurate, precise, consistent, relevant, deep, or broad for our purposes.

We don't achieve excellence in thinking with no end in view. We design for a reason. We fashion and create knowing what we are trying to fashion and create. We originate and produce with a sense of why we are doing so. Thinking that is random, that roams aimlessly through half-formed images, that meanders without an organizing goal, is neither creative nor critical.

This is true because when the mind thinks aimlessly, its energy and drive are typically low, its tendency is generally inert, its results usually barren. What is aimless is also normally pointless and moves in familiar alliance with indolence and dormancy. But when thinking takes on a challenging task, the mind must come alive, ready itself for intellectual labor, engage the intellect in some form of work upon some intellectual object — until such time as it succeeds in originating, formulating, designing, engendering, creating, or producing what is necessary for the achievement of its goal. Intellectual work is essential to creating intellectual products, and that work, that production, presupposes *intellectual standards* judiciously applied. When this happens, creativity and criticality are interwoven into one seamless fabric.

Like the body, the mind has its own form of *fitness* or excellence. Like the body, that fitness is caused by and reflected in activities performed in accordance with standards (criticality). A fit mind can engage successfully in designing, fashioning, formulating, originating, or producing intellectual products worthy of its challenging ends. To achieve this fitness, the mind must learn to take charge of itself, energize itself, press forward when difficulties emerge, proceed slowly and methodically when meticulousness is necessary, immerse itself in a task, become attentive, reflective, and engrossed, circle back on a train of thought, recheck to ensure that it has been thorough, accurate, exact, and deep.

Its *generative power* (creativity) and its *judiciousness* (criticality) can be separated only artificially. In the process of actual thought, they are one. Such thought is systematic — when being systematic serves its end. It also can cast system aside and ransack its intuitions for a lead — when no clear maneuver, plan, strategy, or tactic comes to mind. And the generative, the productive, the creative mind has standards for what it generates and produces. It is not a mind lacking judiciousness, discernment, and judgment. It is not a mind incapable of acuteness and exactness. It is not a mind whose standards are vagueness, imprecision, inaccuracy, irrelevance, triviality, inconsistency, superficiality, and narrowness. The fit mind generates and produces precisely because it has high standards for itself, because it cares about how and what it creates.

Serious thinking originates in a commitment to grasp some truth, to get to the bottom of something, to make accurate sense of that about which it is thinking. This figuring out cannot simply be a matter of arbitrary creation or production. Specific restraints and requirements must be met, something outside the will to which the will must bend, some unyielding objectivity we must painstakingly take into account. This severe, inflexible, stern reality is exactly what forces intellectual criticality and productivity into one seamless whole. If there were no objectivity outside our process of figuring out, we would have literally nothing to figure out. If what we figure out can be anything we want it to be, anything we fantasize it as being, there would be no logic to the expression "figure out."

In a sense, of course, all minds create and produce in a manner reflective of their fitness or lack thereof. Minds indifferent to standards and disciplined judgment tend to judge inexactly, inaccurately, inappropriately, prejudicially. Prejudices, hate, irrational jealousies and fears, stereotypes and misconceptions — these, too, are created, produced, originated by minds. Without minds to produce them, they would not exist. Yet they are not the products of creative minds. They reflect an undisciplined, uncritical mode of thinking and therefore are not properly thought of as products of creativity. In short, except in rare circumstances, creativity presupposes criticality, and criticality creativity. This essential insight is often missed or obscured.

At this point we will focus on the most important sense of creativity in thinking, the sense of thinking as a making, as a process of creating thought, as a process that brings thoughts into being to organize, shape, interpret, and make sense of the world — thinking that, once developed, enables us to achieve goals, accomplish purposes, solve problems, and settle important issues we face as humans in a world in which rapid change is becoming one of the few constants.

A mind that does not systematically and effectively embody intellectual criteria and standards is not disciplined in reasoning things through. Such a mind is not creative. There is, in other words, a reciprocal logic to both intellectual creation and critical judgment. There is an intimate interrelation between the intellectual *making* of things and the ongoing *critique* of that making. Let us examine this reciprocal logic more closely, through some examples.

Painters alternate the application of small amounts of paint to a canvas with the act of stepping back to appraise or assess their work. There are hundreds of acts of assessment that accompany hundreds of brush strokes. In a parallel fashion dancers use mirrors in the studio to observe their dancing while they are dancing. They use what they see in the mirrors as data to assess their performance. They engage in hundreds of acts of assessment in the light of images their minds form as they dance. They practice with a conception in their minds of what they are striving to create. They then assess the gap between the conception they are aiming at and the performance they see. They both create and assess their dancing. Let us now generalize this principle to all thinking as such.

Thinking That Grasps the Logic of Things

To be intellectually assessed and validated, all intellectual products require some logic, some order or coherence, some intellectual structure that makes sense and is rationally defensible. This is true whether one is talking of poems or essays, paintings or choreographed dances, histories or anthropological reports, experiments or scientific theories, philosophies or psychologies,

accounts of specific events or those of general
phenomena or laws.

A product of intellectual work that makes no
sense, that cannot be rationally analyzed and
assessed, that cannot be incorporated into other
intellectual work, or used — and hence that cannot
play a role in any academic tradition or discipline
— is unintelligible. Whether we are designing a
new screwdriver, figuring out how to deal with
our children's misbehavior, or working out a perspective on religion, we must
order our ideas into a system of meanings that make sense to us, a system of
meanings with a coherent logic (which we both create and assess).

> **All thought involves systems of meanings. Thinking should assess what it creates.**

Reasoning As a Creative Act

In the broad sense, all thinking is thinking within a system, and when we have
not yet learned a given system — for example, not yet learned the logic of the
internal combustion engine, the logic of right triangles, or the logic of dolphin
behavior — our minds must bring that system into being, create it in the
fabric, within the structure, of our established ways of thinking. Hence, when
we are thinking something through for the first time, to some extent we are
creating the logic we are using. We are bringing into being new articulations
of our purposes and of our reasons. We are making new assumptions. We
are forming new concepts. We are asking new questions. We are making new
inferences. We are working out our point of view in a direction entirely new to
us.

Indeed, there is a sense in which all reasoned thinking, all genuine acts of
figuring out anything whatsoever, even something previously figured out, is
a new *making*, a new series of creative acts, for we rarely recall our previous
thought whole cloth. Instead, we remember only some part of what we figured
out and we figure out the rest anew (based on the logic of that part and other
logical structures more immediately available to us). Or we modify our existing
ideas by accommodating what we believe to new information we learn. We
continually create new understandings and re-create old understandings
through a similar process of figuring.

Think of the process by which an anthropologist, discovering just one bone
from an animal, is able to deduce, and thus create, the other bones and the

**Every
genuine act
of figuring
out anything
is a new
making, a
new series of
creative acts.**

rest of the body of the animal in question. The human mind continually uses some meanings to create others. Meanings, like living things, are found in systems. They do not stand alone in the mind. They are not like marbles in a bag, each marble independent of all the others. They are like bodily systems — the digestive system, the nervous system, the respiratory system, and so forth. They work together in relation to each other.

To understand the intimate interplay between creative and critical thinking, between the thinking that creates a set of logically interrelated meanings and the thinking that assesses the logic being created, we need to understand, at least in part, how the mind creates meaning.

Whenever we are trying to figure something out, at least three systems are involved:

1.   The logic to be figured out (the system we are trying to understand or create in our minds)
2.   The logic we use to do the figuring (chosen by us from the systems we have already learned or created in our minds)
3.   The logic that results, in the end, from our reasoning — and that has to be assessed for its fit, for the extent to which it has captured the system (1) to be figured out.

One may use, for example, one's understanding of the major themes in a D.H. Lawrence novel (say, *Sons and Lovers*) as an initial framework for understanding the themes of another (say, *Lady Chatterley's Lover*). The resulting understanding may or may not make sense of the actual story. The logic one forges may be inadequate. Or, again, in studying history, one may use one's understanding of the logic behind an economic crisis (say, that of the 1930s in the USA) to understand the logic behind another economic crisis (say, that of the 1990s in the USA). The mental reconstruction one creates may or may not make sense of the logic of what was actually going on economically in the 1990s. In all our learning, we mentally create provisional models (small-scale logical systems) for figuring out what we are trying to learn (the system we are trying to grasp). We then end up with a product of thought, a system we have created. That system may or may not match reality.

Creative Genius — An Exception?

Some might object to the line of reasoning we have laid out thus far. They might say that the intimate interconnection of critical thinking and creative thinking does not hold for truly creative geniuses. They might argue that creative genius emerges spontaneously and mysteriously, that it is linked to unconscious processes that defy rational explanation, processes that go beyond critical thinking and rational thought. As cases in point, they might cite the work of great artists, inventors, and thinkers such as Leonardo Da Vinci, Rembrandt, Michelangelo, Mozart, Beethoven, Wagner, Edison, Shakespeare, Einstein, Newton, and Darwin.

History teaches us that great minds require cultivation and committed intellectual work.

To think-through the relationship between creative genius and critical thought and respond to these objections, let us consider the following questions:

- To what extent is the capacity for creative genius realized in a purely untutored state?
- To what extent must genius be cultivated through the development of critical thought?

We will briefly approach these questions first conceptually, and then historically.

Language as a Guide

Let us look, first at how language sheds light on genius and related concepts.

The *Oxford English Dictionary* defines genius in two ways:

1. As having "natural aptitude, ability or capacity; quality of mind; the special endowments which fit a man for his peculiar work."

2. As "native intellectual power of an exalted type, such as is attributed to those who are esteemed greatest in any department of art, speculation, or practice; instinctive creation, original thought, invention or discovery."

The first definition comes close to what is typically meant by the term gifted, and it implies that the gift predisposes one to high-quality thought within a specialty. The second sense focuses on the successful use of intellectual processes, and primarily on creative production, which need not imply inborn talent.

To better understand the concept of *genius*, let us remind ourselves of its most basic meaning, as well as the meanings of some related concepts: talent, giftedness, aptitude, intelligence, brilliance, accomplishment, proficiency, and virtuosity. Consider the following definitions (and distinctions) found in *Webster's New World Dictionary*:

- **Talent:** implies an apparently native ability for a specific pursuit and connotes either that it is or can be cultivated (or left largely undeveloped) by the one possessing it.
- **Gifted:** suggests that a special ability is bestowed upon one, as by nature, and not acquired through effort.
- **Aptitude:** implies a natural inclination for a particular work, specifically as pointing to a special fitness for or probable success in it.
- **Genius:** implies an inborn mental endowment, specifically of a creative or inventive kind in the arts or sciences, or that is exceptional or phenomenal.
- **Intelligent:** implies the ability to learn or understand from experience or to respond successfully to a new experience.
- **Brilliant:** implies an unusually high degree of intelligence.
- **Accomplished:** skilled, proficient.
- **Proficient:** highly competent, skilled, adept.
- **Virtuoso:** a person displaying great technical skill in some fine art, especially in the performance of music.

Genius is better understood in relation to talent, giftedness, aptitude, capacity, ability, and intelligence.

Notice that talent, gift, genius, and aptitude all imply an inborn disposition to excel within some domain of thought. But intelligence, brilliance, accomplishment, proficiency, and virtuosity need not presuppose innate tendencies. Assuming that these distinctions mirror important qualities in human development, a real possibility is suggested: A person may be highly creative, even brilliant, without having a high degree of innate talent. This possibility is borne out by empirical fact. Many highly accomplished thinkers, rightly considered geniuses, have displayed that brilliance only after investing years in perfecting potential not extraordinary to begin with.

The Narrow-Minded Genius

Before we elaborate this point, let us come to terms with the fact that genius can exist in a highly circumscribed form. At one and the same time, a person can combine "genius" (in one domain of life) with narrowness and parochialism (in all of the others). For example, many brilliant thinkers enthusiastically served in the Nazi regime. The brilliant rocket scientist Werner Von Braun was one such person. The German generals Rommel and Guderian were two others. Within their specialties they functioned at the very highest levels, yet their ethical reasoning abilities and world perspective were sadly impoverished. One-dimensionality is possible in the life of a genius, as in anyone else. Individuals can perform at what appears to be genius level in one domain while thinking superficially in most other domains of their lives.

> **Genius is often specialized, limited to particular intellectual domains.**

Consider the case of Michael Kearney.[1] Kearney graduated from high school at the age of 6, graduated from a junior college at age 8, and completed a bachelor's degree at age 10. Kearney, who earned a master's degree in microbiology at age 14, is at the time of this writing (age 19) working toward a doctorate.

He works as an intern at Microsoft Corporation. According to a newspaper article, Kearney, who is dating a 22-year-old English major, said, "The good thing is we never need to have intellectual debates because I know nothing about Jane Austen." Kearney also said he hasn't given up his dream — to be a TV game-show host. With all his intellect, he'd like nothing better than to fill in for Bob Barker if he retires from "The Price Is Right." "In the back of my head, Hollywood is always calling," said Kearney, who has appeared on talk shows and did a pilot for a talk show. But Kearny hasn't ruled out the possibility of a teaching career or a permanent job with Microsoft, which he said is "pretty cool."

Clearly, Kearny is a person endowed with inborn intellectual gifts that few could boast. Yet what a waste that a genius — or potential genius, if you will — finds satisfaction in the fact that he knows nothing about Jane Austen and aspires, as his highest goal, to become a Hollywood game-show host.

---

1   The *Santa Rosa Press Democrat*, August 11, 2003.

This is just one of the many examples illuminating the fact that, without development of critical capacities, raw inborn talent is easily wasted or misused. The cultivation of innate gifts must be joined with critical thinking skills and abilities if one is to achieve results worthy of high praise.

The Interplay Among Inborn Gifts, Environment, and Self-Motivation

What, then, distinguishes those who excel at creative thought from those who don't? Our analysis implies that outstanding creative work ultimately emerges from application involving both criticality and originality. We concede the obvious: a minimal level of inborn capacity is necessary for high achievement. But one might well become an eminent thinker without inborn genius or extraordinary gifts if moderate raw capacity is joined with intellectual perseverance, intellectual stimulation, and intellectual discipline.

To be more precise, three conditions contribute to a high level of creative thought:

1. A minimal level of innate intellectual capacity (though it need not be extraordinary).
2. An environment that stimulates the development of that capacity.
3. A positive response and inner motivation on the part of the person thus born and situated.

External support and internal motivation are required to foster innate capacity.

We will now support this view with anecdotal evidence that we believe is representative of the role that intellectual discipline, external support, and internal commitment typically play in the development of great thinkers, artists, dancers, and composers. In each case, notice how much attention, tutoring, dedication, and special training each of these thinkers had. Clearly, in the geniuses that we focus on here, much more was involved in their success than innate capacity per se.

Aristotle

According to the *Encyclopedia Britannica* (Eleventh Edition, 1910),

> Aristotle from the first profited by having a father who, being physician to Amyntas II, king of Macedon, and one of the Asclepiads who, according to Galen, practiced their sons in dissection, both prepared the way for his son's influence at the Macedonian court, and gave him a bias to medicine and biology, which certainly led to his belief in nature and natural science, and perhaps induced him to practice medicine… At Athens in his second period for some twenty years he acquired the further advantage of balancing natural science by metaphysics and morals in the course of reading Plato's writings and of hearing Plato's written dogmas. He was an earnest, appreciative, independent student… In his library [Aristotle was] constantly referring to his autograph rolls; entering references and cross-references; correcting, rewriting, collecting and arranging them according to their subjects; showing as well as reading them to his pupils, but with his whole soul concentrated on being and truth (p. 501).

According to Adler, [2]

> Aristotle studied under Plato for 20 years, evolving from a "gifted student to a leading philosopher probing the nature of reality, knowledge, logic and causality… Aristotle eventually—after the age of 50— produced a series of books that form the foundation of biology… He spent years patiently observing, studying, and dissecting animals. In all he described nearly 600 species…over the course of many years, he compiled similarities and differences, noted signs of close or distant relationships and tried to make out nature's own groupings…{he offered} himself as the model — the first and one of the best – of a naturalist at work. He created biology as a science, asked profound questions, and showed that those questions could be answered, but only through patient and painstaking dialogue with nature itself (pp. 22-24).

Ludwig Van Beethoven

As detailed in the the *Encyclopedia Americana*, 1950 edition, The Dutch "van" in Beethoven's name indicates:

> his descent from a family in the Netherlands, the world's musical center in the 15th and 16th centuries… Beethoven's grandfather was a bass singer and a conductor; his father was a tenor…He personally taught Beethoven

2 *Science Firsts: From the Creation of Science to the Science of Creation*, by R. Adler (Hoboken, NJ: John Wiley & Sons, 2002).

to play the violin and the clavier. A sketchbook was always in [Beethoven's] pocket, and into this he jotted his ideas as they came. Afterward he revised and re-revised these sketches. There is hardly a bar in his music of which it may not be said with confidence that it has been rewritten a dozen times. Of the air 'O Hoffnung' in 'Fidelio,' the sketch book shows 18 attempts, and of the concluding chorus 10. These sketches…give an interesting and instructive insight into the workshop of genius (p. 436-437).

Marie Curie

In 1897, Marie Currie began her doctoral research, focusing on a new type of ray existing in uranium. According to Adler,[3]

From the start, her work was precise, systematic, and insightful… With her typical determination, Marie set out to prove the existence of the new element or elements…she repeatedly dissolved and re-crystallized the solutions. Over time, and with great effort, she was able to extract minute quantities of two new, intensely radioactive elements… It meant three years of exhausting labor in an unheated warehouse, stirring huge vats of boiling chemicals with a heavy iron paddle—then painstakingly crystallizing and re-crystallizing the solutions. 'I would be broken with fatigue at the day's end,' she said…Marie Currie…kept her place in the forefront of the field. Marie became the first woman to receive the Nobel Prize (pp. 108-109).

Leonardo Da Vinci

According to *Funk and Wagnall's New Encyclopedia* (1986), Da Vinci was

"the son of a wealthy Florentine notary and a peasant woman. In the mid 1460s the family settled in Florence, where Leonardo was given the best education that Florence, the intellectual and artistic center of Italy, could offer." At the age of 16, Leonardo "was apprenticed as a garzone (studio boy) to Andrea del Verrocchio, the leading Florentine painter and sculptor of his day." As a scientist, Leonardo "understood better than anyone of his century or the next, the importance of precise scientific observation… In anatomy he studied the circulation of the blood and action of the eye. He made discoveries in meteorology and geology, learned the effect of the moon on the tides, foreshadowed modern conceptions of continent formations, and surmised the nature of fossil fuel… (p. 65)." These abilities were clearly developed through systematic and disciplined study.

----

3   ibid.

Galileo

According to the *Encyclopedia Americana* (1950),

> Galileo's father was an impoverished nobleman of Florence, caused him to be instructed in Latin and Greek, drawing and music... In 1581 Galileo entered the University of Pisa, to attend lectures on medicine and the Aristotelian philosophy. Here he became conspicuous in refusing to accept without question the dogmatic statements of his teachers (pp. 237-238).

According to Adler, in 1609, Galileo

> broke through the boundaries of what was known and believed by fashioning a simple telescope and turning it to the skies...Galileo set out to prove or disprove competing theories not just through logic but through experimentation...{He} painstakingly timed balls rolling down inclined planes... With the zeal of a bloodhound hot on a trail, Galileo pushed on with his telescopic observations. By the fall of 1610 he had made close to 100 telescopes... Galileo was the first to carry out real-world experiments — dropping and rolling various weights... which founded the scientific study of motion and gravity (pp. 44-48).

Michelangelo

According to *Funk and Wagnall's New Encyclopedia* (1986),

> At the age of 13, Michelangelo was placed by his father in the workshop of the painter Domenico Chirlandaio. After about two years, he went on to study at the sculpture school in the Medici gardens. In order to prepare to paint the Sistine Chapel ceiling, he drew numerous figure studies and cartoons, devising scores of figure types and poses (pp. 273-274).

The Encyclopedia Britannica: (Eleventh Edition, 1910), adds the following details about Michelangelo's life:

> at thirteen he got himself articled as a paid assistant in the workshop of the brothers Ghirlandaio. Domenico Ghirlandaio had become by this time the foremost painter of Florence. In his service the young Michelangelo laid the foundation of that skill in fresco with which twenty years afterwards he confounded his detractors in Rome. He studied also in the Brancacci chapel, where the frescoes of Masaccio, painted some sixty years before... For nearly all his great life-works preparatory sketches and studies by the master's hand exist. These, with a large number of other drawings, finished and unfinished, done for their own sakes and not for any ulterior use, are of infinite value and interest to the student. Michelangelo was

the most learned and scientific as well as the most inspired and daring of draughtsmen, and from boyhood to extreme old age never ceased to practice with pen, chalk or pencil... Michelangelo's poetic style is strenuous and concentrated like the man. He wrote with labour and much self-correction; we seem to feel him flinging himself on the material of language with the same overwhelming energy and vehemence with which contemporaries describe him as flinging himself on the material of marble — the same impetuosity of temperament combined with the same fierce desire of perfection (pp. 362-368).

The Questioning Minds of Newton, Darwin, and Einstein

Newton, Darwin, and Einstein exemplify the importance of questioning and commitment in developing genius.

Let's take a closer look at the thinking of three of the greatest minds in science history: Newton, Darwin, and Einstein. What Newton, Darwin, and Einstein had in common was not some set of inexplicable or esoteric qualities but, rather, down-to-earth excellence in the art of questioning and an uncommon doggedness in pursuing deep answers to the questions they raised. A close examination of their intellectual development does not suggest mystery but, instead, the importance of focusing on what is fundamental and significant in a subject. Through skilled deep and persistent questioning, they redesigned our view of the physical world and the universe. The questions they raised and the manner in which they pursued these questions embodied the very essence of critical and creative thought.

Isaac Newton[4]

Uninterested in the set curriculum at Cambridge, Newton at age 19 drew up a list of questions under 45 headings. His title, *Quaestiones*, signaled his goal: to constantly question the nature of matter, place, time, and motion. His style was distinctly non-esoteric: to slog his way to knowledge. For example, he "bought Descartes's *Geometry* and read it by himself. After two or three pages, when

---

4   All quotes from *Newton: The Life of Isacc Newton*, by Richard Westfall (New York, NY: Cambridge University Press, 1993).

he could understand no farther, "he began again and advanced farther and continued doing so till he made himself master of the whole."

When asked how he had discovered the law of universal gravitation, he said: "By thinking on it continually, I keep the subject constantly before me and wait till the first dawnings open slowly, by little and little, into a full and clear light." This pattern of consistent, almost relentless questioning, this combination of critical and creative thought, led to depth of understanding and reconstruction of previous theories about the universe.

Newton acutely recognized knowledge as a vast field to be discovered: "I don't know what I may seem to the world, but, as to myself, I seem to have been only like a boy playing on the sea shore, and diverting myself in now and then finding a smoother pebble or prettier shell than ordinary, whilst the great ocean of truth lay all undiscovered before me."

Charles Darwin[5]

Like Newton and Einstein, Darwin had a careful mind rather than a quick one: "I have as much difficulty as ever in expressing myself clearly and concisely; and this difficulty has caused me a very great loss of time, but it has had the compensating advantage of forcing me to think long and intently about every sentence, and thus I have been led to see errors in reasoning and in my own observations or those of other."

In pursuing intellectual questions, Darwin relied upon perseverance and continual reflection, rather than memory and quick reflexes. "I have never been able to remember for more than a few days a single date or line of poetry." Instead, he had "the patience to reflect or ponder for any number of years over any unexplained problem...At no time am I a quick thinker or writer: whatever I have done in science has solely been by long pondering, patience, and industry".

Albert Einstein[6]

For his part, Einstein, did so poorly in school that when his father asked his son's headmaster what profession his son should adopt, the answer was simply, "It doesn't matter; he'll never make a success of anything." In high school, the

---

5   Quotes from *The Autobiography of Charles Darwin*, ed. by Francis Darwin (New York, NY: Dover Publications, 1958).

6   Quotes taken from *A. Einstein: The Life and Times*, by Ronald Clark (New York, NY: Avon Books, 1984); and *A Variety of Men*, by C.P. Snow (New York, NY: Charles Scribners and Sons, 1967).

regimentation "created in him a deep suspicion of authority. This feeling lasted all his life, without qualification."

Einstein showed no signs of being a genius, and as an adult denied that his mind was extraordinary: "I have no particular talent. I am merely extremely inquisitive." He failed his entrance examination to the Zurich Polytechnic. When he finally passed, the examinations so constrained his mind that, when he had graduated, he did not want to think about scientific problems for a year. His final exam was so nondistinguished that afterward he was refused a post as an assistant (the lowest grade of postgraduate job). Exam-taking, then, was not his forte. Thinking critically and creatively were.

Einstein had the basic critical thinking ability to cut problems down to size: "One of his greatest intellectual gifts, in small matters as well as great, was to strip off the irrelevant frills from a problem."

When we consider the work of these three thinkers, Newton, Darwin, and Einstein, we find not the unfathomable, genius mind but, rather, thinkers who combined critical and creative thought in the passionate, but non-esoteric, pursuit of truth.

Creativity — Not Mystified

A careful examination of the history of creative people, we believe, supports our central claim that critical and creative thought are intimately related. Each without the other is of limited use. Creativity without criticality is mere novelty. Criticality without creativity is bare negativity. Native giftedness cannot be developed without some cultivation and environmental support. For example,

Creativity is best understood in simple everyday thought.

Einstein never could have become one of the world's greatest scientists had he been born to a sub-Saharan mother living in absolute poverty. Through cultivation and support, both judiciousness and originality must be encouraged — not to mention the intellectual courage and perseverance that enable persons of great talent to study and develop through many years of challenging intellectual work.

The material point here is that creativity should not be mystified. Much of what appears to be inexplicable can be explained — at least in large part — by mundane accounts. Even those born with extraordinary gifts need the corrective and expansive power of critical thought. Without the analytic tools of critical thinking (tools that enable a thinker to plumb the structure of knowledge), one will have a limited grasp of any given field of knowledge as a system of thought. Without a grasp of the structure of knowledge and its systemic functions, one will have difficulty transferring knowledge from one context to another. Without the intellectual standards of critical thinking, one is apt to overstate the strengths of one's thought and underestimate its limitations. Without the activated knowledge that critical thinking empowers, we are unlikely to be personally transformed by our learning. Without the cultivation of our intellectual capacities such as fairmindedness, we are unlikely to notice our inconsistencies and contradictions. We are apt to uncritically conform in many domains of our personal lives.

Each and every one of us is born with mental hard-wiring over which we have no control. But, no matter what our raw capacity at birth, that capacity must be cultivated over time if we are to reach our potential. Creativity requires the expansive empowerment of sound critical thought. Critical thought requires the will to create and improve.

The Elements of Thought

One way to summarize the essence of critical thinking is as follows:

Critical thinking is the art of thinking about thinking in such a way as to:
1. identify its strengths and weaknesses, and
2. recast it in improved form (where necessary).

The first characteristic requires the thinker to be skilled in analytic and evaluative thinking. The second requires the thinker to be skilled in creative thinking. Thus, critical thinking has three dimensions: the analytic, the evaluative, and the creative. Though we separate these functions for purposes of theoretical clarity, we nevertheless argue that each must be involved if the other two are to be effective.

Critical thinking cannot be understood separate from its power to deconstruct thinking into elements. Once we see clearly the constituent parts of our thinking, we can better assess them. Then, having assessed the constituent parts, we are in a position to raise thinking to a higher level (the creative dimension of critical thought). One analyzes to assess; one assesses to improve.

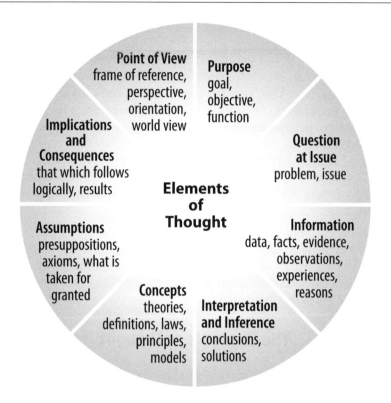

Here are each of the creative acts implicit in analytic thought.

1. **Purpose, goal, or end in view:** Whenever we reason, we reason to some end, to achieve some purpose, to satisfy some desire or fulfill some need. One source of problems in reasoning is traceable to defects at the level of goal, purpose, or end. If we create goals that are unrealistic or contradictory to other goals we have, the reasoning we use to achieve our goals is problematic.

2. **Question at issue (or problem to be solved):** Whenever we attempt to reason, there is at least one question at issue, at least one problem to be solved. One area of concern for the reasoner therefore should be the creation or formulation of the question to be answered or problem to be solved. If we are not clear about the question we are asking, or how the question relates to our basic purpose or goal, we will not be able to find a reasonable answer to it, or an answer that will serve our purpose. As

originators of our questions, we are authors of our own vagueness, muddle, or clarity.

3. **Point of view or frame of reference:** Whenever we reason, we must reason within some point of view or frame of reference. This point of view or frame of reference is created by the mind. Any defect in our point of view or frame of reference is a possible source of problems in our reasoning. Our point of view may be too narrow or too parochial, may be based on false or misleading analogies or metaphors, may not be precise enough, may contain contradictions, and so forth. Whatever qualities are inherent in our point of view, they are the result of the engendering acts of our own mind. Points of view are not given in nature; they are constructed (i.e. created) by human minds.

4. **The information we use in reasoning:** Whenever we reason, we are reasoning about some stuff, some phenomena. Any defect in the experiences, data, evidence, or raw material upon which our reasoning is based is a possible source of problems. We must actively decide which of a myriad of possible experiences, data, and evidence, we will use. These decisions are a creation of our minds at work. Information is not given by nature, it is constructed (i.e. created) by human minds.

5. **The conceptual dimension of our reasoning:** All reasoning uses some ideas or concepts and not others — ideas or concepts created by the mind. Any defect in the concepts or ideas (including the theories, principles, axioms, or rules) with which we reason is a possible source of problems. The power or poverty of our ideas is a direct result of the quality of our thought. Concepts and ideas are not given to us by nature. They are constructs (i.e. creations) of human minds.

6. **Assumptions — the starting points of reasoning:** All reasoning must begin somewhere, and must take some things for granted. Any defect in the starting points of our reasoning, any problem in what we are taking for granted, is a possible source of problems. Only we can create the assumptions on the basis of which we will reason. We construct (i.e. create) our minds' starting points.

7. **Our inferences, interpretations and conclusions:** Reasoning proceeds by steps called inferences. To make an inference is to think as follows: "Because this is so, that also is so (or probably so)." Any defect in the inferences we make while we reason presents a possible problem in our reasoning. Information, data, and situations do not determine what we shall deduce from them. We create inferences, interpretations, and

conclusions using the concepts and assumptions we bring to situations by the powers of origination of our own minds. Inferences exist only in minds. They are meaning-making constructions (i.e. creations).

8. **Implications and consequence — where our reasoning takes us:**
All reasoning begins somewhere and then proceeds somewhere else. No reasoning is static. Thus, our reasoning has implications, ideas that follow from our reasoning, things that might happen if we reason in this or that way, if we make this or that decision. Consequences are the actual results of our acting upon our reasoning. The implications of our reasoning are an implicit creation of our reasoning. The mind must be able to figure out what might happen if this or that action is taken in this or that situation. This figuring out is a creative act of the mind. Any problem in thinking through implications implies a problem in creative thought.

Intellectual Standards

To be effective thinkers, we must go beyond taking thinking apart. We also must apply standards to assess our thinking. Intellectual standards ultimately derive from the nature of thought itself and what we characteristically need thought to do.

Only when we construct and use intellectual standards can we effectively assess thinking.

Thus, the intellectual standard of clarity derives from the fact that we want or need to communicate a certain meaning to others and unclear language undermines or defeats that purpose. The intellectual standard of accuracy derives from the fact that we are trying to understand or communicate things as they actually are. Inaccurate thought defeats that purpose. The intellectual standard of precision derives from the fact that we often need details and specifics to accomplish our purpose. Imprecision, or the failure to provide details and specifics, defeats that purpose.

The intellectual standard of relevance derives from the fact that some information — however true it might be — does not bear on a question to which we need an answer. Irrelevant information, thrust into the thinking process, diverts us from the information we do need and prevents us from answering the question at hand. To generalize, it would be unintelligible to say, "I want to reason well but I am indifferent as to whether or not my reasoning is clear, precise, accurate, relevant, logical, consistent, or fair."

Questions Focused on Intellectual Standards

Clarity
Could you elaborate further?
Could you give me an example?
Could you illustrate what you mean?

Accuracy
How could we check on that?
How could we find out if that is true?
How could we verify or test that?

Precision
Could you be more specific?
Could you give me more details?
Could you be more exact?

Relevance
How does that relate to the problem?
How does that bear on the question?
How does that help us with the issue?

Depth
What factors make this a difficult problem?
What are some of the complexities of this question?
What are some of the difficulties we need to deal with?

Breadth
Do we need to look at this from another perspective?
Do we need to consider another point of view?
Do we need to look at this in other ways?

Logic
Does all this make sense together?
Does your first paragraph fit in with your last?
Does what you say follow from the evidence?

Significance
Is this the most important problem to consider?
Is this the central idea to focus on?
Which of these facts are most important?

Fairness
Do I have any vested interest in this issue?
Am I sympathetically representing the
    viewpoints of others?

A similar point can be made about concepts and words implicit in educated usage. It would be unintelligible — unless very special circumstances were to prevail — to say, "I am trying to determine whether or not I am a selfish person, but I am not concerned with what the word selfish implies." The logic of the question, "Is Jack a selfish person?" is implicit in the established use of the word *selfish*. Unless we have a good reason to stipulate a special meaning for a term, we need to apply terms in keeping with educated usage, and thus to be accurate in our use of words.

It is through careful application of intellectual standards to our thinking that we create high-quality reasoning. Without these standards, our thinking is likely to wander. We then lack direction for our creations. We then are unable to distinguish high- and low-quality reasoning. In short, creative thought presupposes adherence to intellectual standards. Consider the absurdity of saying: "My thinking is highly creative; the only problem is that it is also unclear, inaccurate, imprecise, irrelevant, superficial, narrow, illogical, and trivial."

Critical Thinking Applied to the Arts

We have argued that to evaluate products of reasoning, we need to acquire intellectual standards. But what about creative products that emerge through artistic thought? To what extent, if any, is critique or critical analysis an intrinsic part of artistic thought and work? Some argue that art is not to be assessed at all, or not, at least, with any rational process. Some argue that art objects are sui generis, that each is individual and its nature ineffable, that the beauty of art cannot be captured in words.

Yet artists themselves often argue the strengths and weaknesses of art objects. Some art objects are praised. Some are condemned. Some are both praised and condemned (by different persons). Not every art object is highly valued and praised. Some art goes into museums and art schools. Some is cast into garbage bins. Thus, if we believe that there is such a thing as great art, we had better be prepared to justify our claims with words to the point (and examples aplenty).

Art criticism, then, plays a prominent role in art. If we take the position that anything goes within art, it follows that art is not worthy of praise. It is anything and everything and nothing. If high achievement in art cannot be identified or defined, it cannot, without self-contradiction, be said to exist.

And although art critics disagree about what standards are most important in assessing art, there does seem to be a core set of general standards that define all great works of art, for every artistic masterpiece is considered to have significant, universal, and enduring value. The standards of significance, universality, and enduring value, then, are minimal criteria that define great works of art. Of course, how to apply these standards may, in some cases, give rise to a debate among well-informed students of art.

It should also be recognized that any reasoning about art must be assessed in accordance with the intellectual standards that apply to all reasoning. The quality of reasoning about art — about its features, the processes that produce the art, its history, its role in society, its importance, its purpose, its message — must be assessed in the same way that disciplined thinkers assess the quality of reasoning about numbers, plants, relationships, architecture — indeed about anything whatsoever.

Beyond universal intellectual standards, there are subject-specific standards to which thinkers must adhere in any discipline, including art. Chemists are expected to adhere to chemical standards, historians to historical standards, sociologists to sociological standards, and artists to artistic standards. Thus, there are art-specific standards for assessing poetry, painting, drawing, plays, novels, and, indeed, any artistic product. Of course, the application of specific standards to specific art objects is sometimes a matter of intense debate among experts.

Creative production must be critically assessed.

Many art standards are identifiable and intuitive to the skilled artist. For example, in pictorial composition, some candidate fundamental principles are:

1. **Dominance**, which requires that there be one object or center in a picture of major interest, to which all other objects are subordinate;

2. **Opposition**, which requires that the various elements in a picture show contrast and variety of line, shape and value;

3. **Balance**, which requires that these contrasts create a harmonious effect.

Art critics would likely agree on a core of great works of art, art created by artists such as Michelangelo, Mozart, Beethoven, Rembrandt, Van Gogh, Milton, Shakespeare, Pope, Keats, Dostoyevsky, and Tolstoi. But beyond some given core, critique is often highly contentious, the paradigms within which critics think so different, that one cannot reconcile the contrasting views. And what is sometimes considered creativity within the arts can become so esoteric that its defense and critique border on the unintelligible.

It is easy to satirize the radically subjective use of art standards by those who pretend to artistic sensitivity and judgment while lacking depth of understanding. Consider the following discussion from Woody Allen's movie Manhattan. In this scene, Isaac (Woody Allen) and his girlfriend Tracy meet Isaac's best friend and his "intellectual" girlfriend, Mary.

ISAAC:	We were downstairs at the photography exhibition…incredible, absolutely incredible!!
MARY:	Really, you liked that?
ISAAC:	The photographs downstairs…great, absolutely great!! Didn't you?
MARY:	No, I really felt that it was very derivative. To me it looked like something straight out of Diane Arbus, but had none of the wit.
ISAAC:	Really, you know, well we didn't like it as much as the Plexiglas sculpture, that I will admit. I mean there…
MARY:	Really, you liked the Plexiglas, huh??
ISAAC:	You didn't like the Plexiglas sculpture either?…
MARY:	Ugh, that's interesting, nuh I ugh…
ISAAC:	Well, it was a hell of a lot better than that steel cube; did you see the steel cube?
TRACY:	Oh, yeah that was the worst.
MARY:	Now that was brilliant to me, absolutely brilliant.
ISAAC:	The steel cube was brilliant?
MARY:	Yeah, to me it was very textural. You know what I mean? It was perfectly integrated, and it had a…a marvelous kind of negative capability. The rest of the stuff downstairs was bullshit.

The above scene is not just funny. It is funny because it comes close to capturing the extent to which otherwise intelligent people sometimes fail to recognize the extent of their ignorance (about art) and confuse glibness with insight.

So what are we saying? For one, even in art, where creativity of the highest degree is essential, critical thinking plays a vital role. Great artists are not uncritical about art, especially about their own art. They typically have a lot to say about what they are striving to achieve and how they are trying to achieve it. And when artists or art critics reason about art, that reasoning must be subject to critical analysis and assessment. Each field of art generates a vocabulary of art-specific standards. Assessment occurs at multiple levels. But in art, as in every other domain of human achievement, criticality and creativity work hand-in-glove, mutually dependent, mutually interacting, mutually influencing each other.

PART II

Critical/Creative Thinking and the Foundations of Meaningfulness

Figuring Out the Logic of Things

As we said at the outset:

> Creative thinking, especially, must be demystified and brought down to earth. For this reason, we deal with it in terms of its highest manifestation in the work of geniuses, and also in its most humble manifestations in ordinary run-of-the-mill perception and thought.

> In learning new concepts, in making sense of our experience, in apprehending a new subject field or language, in reading, writing, speaking, and listening, our minds engage in full-fledged (though commonplace) creative acts. To understand how and why this is so, we need not appeal to the esoteric, the recondite, or the arcane.

In this spirit, let us discuss how the mind operates when figuring things out, how it creates meaning in its everyday functioning, and how that meaning must be assessed for quality.

To say that something is meaningful is to say that it can be understood by use of our reason, that we can form concepts that accurately — though not necessarily thoroughly — characterize the nature of that thing. Only when we have in some way conceptualized a thing can we reason through it. Because nature does not provide us with innate ideas, we must create concepts, individually or socially. Once conceptualized, a thing is integrated by us into a network of ideas (because no concept can stand alone) and, as such, becomes the vehicle for many possible inferences.

In thinking critically, we take command of the meanings we create.

For example, the way I conceptualize marriage guides the conclusions I come to about whether to marry a specific person, and then, later, whether I think my marriage is working, and whether, perhaps, I should seek to dissolve the marriage. Similarly, the way I conceptualize the process of learning guides the conclusions I come to about learning. For example, if I conceptualize learning as the memorizing of facts, and if I am skilled at memorization, I will conclude that I am a skilled learner. I will infer that anyone who is good at memorizing facts is bright, and those who are unskilled at memorizing facts are not. I will infer that the only thing one has to learn well is the skill of memorization. I therefore will misunderstand what learning entails. This misunderstanding is initiated in my erroneous conceptualization of learning.

Once we begin to make inferences about something, we can do so either well or poorly, justifiably or unjustifiably, in keeping with the meaning of the concept and the nature of what we know of the thing conceptualized, or not so in keeping. If we are not careful, we might (and very often do) infer, and thus create in our minds, more than is implied.

If I hear a sound at the door and conceptualize it as "scratching at the door," I may infer that it is my dog wanting to come in. I have used my reason (my creative capacity to conceptualize and infer) to interpret the noise as a "scratch," and I have assumed, in the process, that the only creature in the vicinity who could be making that scratch at my door is my dog. But my reasoning could be off. I might have misinterpreted the noise as a "scratch" (I may even have misheard where the noise was coming from) or I might have wrongly assumed that there were no other creatures around that might make that noise. Notice that in these acts I *create, originate,* or ***bring into being*** the conceptualizations at the root of my thinking.

We approach virtually everything in our experience as something that can be thus decoded by the power of our minds to create a conceptualization and to make inferences on the basis of it (hence to bring into being further conceptualizations). We do this so routinely and automatically that we typically don't recognize ourselves as engaged in processes of reasoned creation — the creations of the reasoning mind. In our everyday life we don't first experience the world in *concept-less* form and then deliberately place what we experience into categories so as to make sense of things.

Rather, it is as if things are given to us with their names inherent in them. Thus, we see trees, clouds, grass, roads, people, men, women, and so on. We apply these concepts intuitively, as if no rational, creative act were involved. Yet, if we think about it, we will realize that there was a time when we had to learn names for things and, hence, before we knew those names, we couldn't possibly have seen these phenomena through the mediation of these concepts.

In learning these concepts, we had to ***create*** them in our own minds out of the concepts we had already learned.

When we say "the logic of something," we mean something basic and simple: ***the system of meanings that makes sense of a thing***. Thus, you must understand certain essential meanings before you can make sense of, for example, how a bicycle operates. When you understand the system behind it, and can explain that system, you then grasp the logic of how a bicycle functions. You might, of course, be able to ride a bicycle, but not understand how it operates.

For example, we study living organisms to construct ***bio-logic*** (biology) — that is, to establish ways to conceptualize and make valid inferences about life forms. We study social arrangements to construct ***socio-logic*** (sociology) — that is, to establish ways to conceptualize and make valid inferences about life in society. We study the historical past to construct the logic of history, ways to conceptualize and make valid inferences about the past. Because no one is born with these conceptual structures at his or her command, everyone must create them. Thus, all humans are creative merely because we are living a human life and, hence, inevitably figuring things out as we go.

In thinking critically, we take command of our conceptual creations, assessing them far more explicitly than is normally done. Concepts, like all human creations, can be well or poorly designed. Critical judgment (discernment, being judicious) is always relevant to the process of design and construction, whether that construction be conceptual or material.

In the remainder of this guide, we explore the two interrelated phases of critical thinking: producing (creating) and assessing (critiquing) systems of meaning. We focus explicitly on:
  • Concepts and language
  • Human thinking
  • Academic disciplines
  • Questions
  • Reading, writing, speaking, and listening

Learning Concepts and Language

In this guide we are using the word *concept* to mean simply a group of things resembling each other in a describable way. We understand conceptualization to be a process by which the mind infers a thing to be of a certain kind, to belong properly to some given class of things. Hence, if I describe someone as clever, I have placed the person into a generalized group of people (those who are quick-witted).

To learn concepts and use language, we must create them through mental acts.

Our minds understand things in terms of how they relate to what we believe to be true. We interpret the world by putting objects into categories or concepts, each of which highlights some set of similarities or differences. We then link the thing with other concepts, in the process validating a certain set of inferences.

For example, if I see a creature before me and take it to be a dog, I can reasonably infer that it will bark rather than meow or purr. Furthermore, by placing it into the concept of dog, I create a family of meanings by means of other concepts interrelated with that of dog, such as animal, furry, muzzle, paw, tail, and so forth.

In learning to speak our native language, we necessarily learn thousands of concepts that, when properly used, enable us to make countless legitimate inferences about the objects of our experience. Unfortunately, nothing in the way we ordinarily learn to speak a language forces us to use concepts carefully, or prevents us from making unjustifiable inferences while engaged in their use. The mind that creates meanings can create them well or poorly. Indeed, a fundamental need for critical thinking is given by the fact that as long as the mind remains undisciplined in its use of concepts, it is susceptible to any number of illegitimate inferences created by egocentric or undisciplined mental acts.

The process of learning the concepts implicit in a natural language such as English is a process of creating facsimiles (in our minds) of the concepts implicit in the language usage to which we are exposed. But we cannot "give" anyone the meaning of a word or phrase; that meaning must be created individually by every person who learns it. We can give a person a dictionary-definition of a word, but that definition must be interpreted and, in effect, paraphrased in the mind to gain initial ownership of it. When we misinterpret a definition, we mis-learn the meaning of the word in question. Thus, we create in our minds a meaning that conflicts with the established meaning of the word.

To take command of our thinking, critically and creatively, requires that we take command of the language we use. Many of our ideas or concepts come from the languages we have learned to speak, and in which we do our thinking. Embedded in the educated use of words are criteria or standards we must respect before we can think clearly and precisely by means of those words. We are free, of course, to use a given word in a special way in special circumstances, but only if we have good reason for modifying its established meaning.

Such special stipulations should proceed from a clear understanding of established educated use. We are not free, for example, to use the word "education" as if it were synonymous with the words "indoctrination," "socialization," or "training." We are not free to equate pride with cunning, truth with belief, knowledge with information, arrogance with self-confidence, desire with love, and so on. Each word has its own established logic, a logic that cannot, without confusion or error, be ignored.

Each word has a home in at least one established system of meanings. To learn the meaning of any one word in a system of words, we have to learn something of the other (interwoven) meanings. We have to re-create that system in our thinking, and we must base that creation on meanings we have created previously. Learning the meaning of a word is not a simple task, because in each case we must create a new concept in our minds out of modified old understandings. This requires that our creation be ordered, restrained, regulated, and controlled. Words do not mean anything we want them to mean. We must construct meanings in our minds that are accurate — given established educated usage. As always, thinking that calls for assessment (criticality) works hand-in-glove with thinking requiring creative production.

Critiquing Human Thinking

In a literal sense there is no virtue in merely creating meaning. Prejudices, self-delusions, distortions, misconceptions, and caricatures — all are products of the mind as maker and creator. Unfortunately, humans typically create thought that is vague, fragmented, contradictory, egocentric, sociocentric, and lacking in foundational insights. This is so because the natural state of the human mind is one of egocentrism. When functioning in such a state, we give free reign to unconscious processes of mind. Language then is used in a self-serving, self-deceptive way. We manipulate to gain advantage. We rationalize to obscure and justify. Our critical capacity to assess and our creative capacity to produce are both misused.

In undisciplined egocentric thought, we do not see ourselves designing, fashioning, or shaping meanings. We do not understand the significant relationship between care and precision in language usage and care and precision in thought. We speak and write in vague sentences because we have no criteria for choosing words other than that some words and not others occur to us. We often fail to put our sentences into intelligible relationships to one another because, for the most part, we do not recognize any responsibility to do so, nor do we have any clear idea of how to do so.

To think well, we must routinely critique our egocentric tendencies and transform irrational thinking into rational thinking.

In the absence of cultivated intellectual discipline, it is difficult to master well-developed or refined sets of conceptual relationships. Significant improvements in human thinking must take place over an extended time and must nurture the ability to move into and out of divergent ways of thinking. We must work our way to intellectual discipline. Only by moving back and forth between undisciplined thought and some set of disciplined understandings can we become intellectually disciplined thinkers. Without critical command of thought, we are unlikely to create ideas of significance.

When people are highly egocentric, their skill in thinking is isolated. They think well only when their egocentric tendencies are not engaged. For example, a person may think egocentrically when relating to family and friends, yet think critically in a profession (as a physicist, architect, or chemist). Expert thinkers in one domain are often irrational and self-deceived in another.

The human mind, then, does not necessarily develop as an integrated whole. This is one of the reasons it is important to learn critical thinking in the most generalized, comprehensive way. When learning to think in one domain of concepts, it is useful to be exposed to logically illuminating examples from other domains.

The creative dimension of human thinking is rarely developed in the absence of disciplined thinking and critical judgment. Humans need comprehensive tools of critical thought to structure our lives productively, to solve the problems we face, and to deal with complex multi-logical issues.

Learning Academic Disciplines

The logic of learning an academic discipline — from the point of view of critical and creative thought — is illuminating. Each academic discipline is a domain of thinking in which humans deploy specialized concepts, and thereby make inferences that follow from, or are suggested by, those concepts. To learn the key concepts in a discipline, we must construct them in our minds by a series of mental acts. We must construct them as an ordered system of relationships. We must construct both foundations and the concepts that derive from those foundations. Each moment of that creation requires discernment and judgment. There is no way to implant, transfer, or inject the system in prefabricated form. It cannot be put on a mental disc and dumped into the mind without an intellectual struggle. Critical judgment is essential to all acts of construction, and all acts of construction are open to critical assessment. We create and assess; we assess *what* we create; we assess as we create.

To learn a discipline, we must create its system in our minds and critically assess the systems we create.

One way to test our rudimentary knowledge of any given system of thought is to attempt to state, elaborate, exemplify, and illustrate the most fundamental concepts within that system. For example, if you believe you understand a given science, you should be able, at minimum, to construct your understanding of what that science is in a way that would satisfy those who have mastered its basic logic. Writing forces the mind to make mental acts explicit. Paraphrasing texts is one way to drive the mind to construct concepts essential to the process of learning. For example, consider what you would learn by executing the following:

- State what a living system is (in one sentence).
- Elaborate on what you have said (in multiple explanatory sentences).
- Construct an extended example of one living system.
- Devise an analogy or a metaphor to illuminate the idea of a living system.

These same four acts of construction can be used to assess someone's basic knowledge of any concept whatsoever. For example, consider using the same processes for explaining and elaborating the concept of democracy, an equation, mass, energy, a chemical reaction, the key problem facing the main character in a story, the main point in a story, and indeed any concept you care to think of. Every subject area has a network or system of concepts that must be constructed in the mind to think successfully within the subject. To learn any subject, we must perform constructive/creative acts. They are a key to taking command of a discipline.

It is often complicated to create understanding of academic disciplines in one's mind because many disciplines are multi-logical. Hence they require conflicting constructions on the learner's part. Within these disciplines individual theories are defended by different, apparently equal, expert proponents. To some extent, of course, questions that call for the adjudication of competing systems emerge in all disciplines. Nevertheless, some disciplines — namely, those that attempt to conceptualize and make sense of human realities — seem to be inescapably multi-logical: history, psychology, sociology, philosophy, anthropology, economics, literature, and the fine arts, to name a few. In these domains, seminal thinkers often develop comprehensive alternative, conflicting views. To understand such a field, one must learn to construct and then reconcile conflicting logics (theories, systems).

Multi-logical reasoning demands exacting and discriminating restraint and self-regulation. In reading, for example, the writings of Freud, Adler, and Jung, I must create in my mind three overlapping systems of thought, systems that are in agreement on some points and disagreement on others. If I come to understand what I have read, I have come to develop the ability to think within three different systems of thought. Once again, creativity and criticality work together. Each individual student, through a process of disciplined intellectual work, must generate, fabricate, and engender in his/her mind Freudian, Adlerian, and Jungian thoughts. Each must create the inner understandings that enable him/her to draw fine distinctions, distinctions that honor the multiple logics they collectively express. Finally, each student must assess the thinking he or she creates.

Questioning

Every question, when well formulated, imposes specific demands on us, demands that emerge from the concepts embedded in the question itself, established usages of those concepts, and the context of the question. If I ask, "What is the sum of 434 and 987?" the question requires an answer that

To conceive and formulate fruitful questions, we must call upon both creativity and criticality.

is entailed by the established meaning of the word "oum." If I ask, "Is Jack your friend or merely an acquaintance?" the question requires an answer in keeping with educated usages of the words "friend" and "acquaintance." If I ask you, "To what extent are you learning to think critically?" the question requires that you (1) understand precisely what is implied by the expression "think critically" and (2) assess your thinking by comparing it to an appropriate standard for determining whether, and to what extent, one is able to think critically.

An appropriate answer to any question, then, is an answer constructed in accordance with the logical demands of the question. Often, however, people are cavalier in their handling of questions — that is, in the way they formulate and go about answering questions. Many are not in the habit of putting their own questions precisely, and, when answering the questions of others, they often respond impressionistically. Thinking without care, discipline, or sensitivity to what is implied by the established logic of the question (or by the context in which the question is asked), their approach to the question is often a puzzle in subjectivity. When called upon to sharpen their questions or to respond more carefully and precisely, many respond with irritation or annoyance, exasperated by the (to them unintelligible) request to be clear or precise or accurate or relevant or consistent.

This general insensitivity to the logic of questions is part of a broader insensitivity to the logic of language, which is itself part of an even broader insensitivity to the need for care and discipline in reasoning, in using concepts, in figuring out the logic of the world within and around us. All of these, in turn, are part of the general insensitivity to the need to discipline our mind's creative productions, to shape them in accord with critically based, restraining conditions — conditions sometimes given by the logic of language, sometimes by the nature of the material world.

Reading, Writing, Speaking, and Listening

To read well, one must actively construct an interpretation, imagine alternative meanings, imagine possible objections and thus think creatively while reading. Beyond that, one has to assess and judge (criticality) when one reads. Reading is not good reading — accurate, clear, plausible — unless it is also critical reading.

The same can be said for writing. With only rudimentary language skills, any one of us can write out our ideas. We can create ideas in written form. But to write well is to formulate in written form ideas that are clear, coherent, and rational. Conversely, writing that lacks discipline, that lacks a critical element, is often vague, confused, muddled, and/or incoherent.

Similarly, those who know the rudimentary forms of a language can speak it. To speak a language well, however, requires clarity and coherence of thought — a clear conception of what one wants to say, the ability to formulate one's thoughts in coherent ideas, and the discipline to adhere to standards of established usage.

Similar points can be made about the art of listening. To listen well, one must be able to accurately summarize what is being said, to create in one's mind the meanings intended by the speaker.

Reading, writing, speaking, and listening are all dialogical, requiring multiple acts of assessment and creativity.

To more fully illustrate our point, we focus in the remainder of this section on reading and its relationship to critical and creative thought. Similar elaborations could be made for writing, speaking, and listening.

The system of meanings within a written piece enters one's thinking only through the system of meanings one brings to the reading process. Without close reading skills, we are limited in our ability to learn. We fail to create intelligible meanings as we read. We fail to assess accurately as we read. We are unable to continually reshape and modify our understandings as we proceed through the text. Only through close reading skills, through mindful interaction with the text, can we create new concepts or internalize new information.

When we read a text, the system of meanings we create through that reading matches the logic of the text. Reading proficiency is both a creative task (a making, a creating) and a critical task (an assessing, a judging). The making and the assessing, the creating and the judging, are integral to one seamless process of sound reasoning. We create the logic of the text in our minds as we conduct a dialogue with it using critical processes. We raise and answer probing questions as we read, generating and fashioning ideas and meanings in and through our responses.

Consider a classic text, the preamble to the Declaration of Independence:

> When in the course of human events it becomes necessary for one people to dissolve the political bands which have connected them with another and to assume among the powers of the earth, the separate and equal station to which the Laws of Nature and of Nature's God entitle them, a decent respect to the opinions of mankind requires that they should declare the causes which impel them to the separation. We hold these Truths to be self-evident, that all men are created equal, that they are endowed by their Creator with certain unalienable Rights, that among these are Life, Liberty, and the pursuit of Happiness…

Only when we have developed close reading skills will we be able to break down this, or indeed any, passage into digestible parts and create a detailed and plausible paraphrase of those parts. Consider the following paraphrase example:

When in the course of human events, it becomes necessary for one people to dissolve the political bands which have connected them with another…

PARAPHRASE: "Political" arrangements (forms of government) are not necessarily permanent, and it is important sometimes to abolish them and set up new arrangements. When this is true, one group of people have to separate themselves from the group with which they were formerly joined.

and to assume among the powers of the earth, the separate and equal station to which the Laws of Nature and of Nature's God entitle them,…

PARAPHRASE: No governments should dominate any other government, but all should have the same status (be "separate and equal"). The thirteen states of the United States of America should stand as a "separate and equal" force in the world. This act of a people declaring themselves independent of other people (with whom they were formerly connected) is a perfectly natural act based on "the Laws of Nature." The thirteen states are "entitled" by natural law to revolt and declare themselves "separate and equal" to all other countries of the world.

a decent respect to the opinions of mankind requires that they should declare the causes which impel them to the separation.

PARAPHRASE: But when a people decide to break away from another people and establish their own nation, they should — out of respect for the views of the other peoples in the world — lay out the reasons that have led them to make the "revolutionary" decision they have made.

We hold these truths to be self-evident, that all men are created equal, that they are endowed by their Creator with certain unalienable Rights, that among these are Life, Liberty, and the pursuit of Happiness.

PARAPHRASE: Some truths are so obvious that everyone should recognize that they are true simply by thinking them through. This includes the truth that every person is just as good as any other, and the truth that every person should be accorded rights so basic that no one should be allowed to deny them. These rights include the right not to be hurt, harmed, or killed; the right to as much freedom (of thought, of movement, of choice of associates, of belief) as is possible; and the right to live one's life as one pleases.

Now consider a comparison of students engaged in reading a text.[7] This example is an episode-by-episode transcript of two students (Steven and Colleen) thinking aloud as they interpret a given passage. The researcher's questions are given in brackets. The commentaries following the student interpretations in each episode are those of the researchers, Norris and Phillips. To simulate the task for you, we present the passage without a title and one episode at a time, as was done with the children. We can see in these two readers a striking difference between high-and low-quality constructions embedded in the act of reading.

---

7   This example is taken from an article by Stephen Norris and Linda Phillips, "Explanation of Reading Comprehension: Scema Theory and Critical Thinking Theory", in *Teacher's Record*, Volume 89, Number 2, Winter 1987.

Episode 1

The stillness of the morning air was broken. The men headed down the bay.

STEVEN: The men were heading down the bay, I'm not sure why yet. It was a very peaceful morning. [Any questions?] No, not really. [Where do you think they're going?] I think they might be going sailing, water skiing, or something like that.

COLLEEN: The men are going shopping. [Why do you say that?] They're going to buy clothes at The Bay. [What is The Bay?] It's a shopping center. [Any questions?] No. [Where do you think they're going?] They're going shopping because it seems like they broke something.

Steven recognizes that information is insufficient for explaining what the men are doing. Upon questioning, he tentatively suggests a couple of alternatives consistent with the information given but indicates there are other possibilities. Colleen presents one explanation of the story and seems fairly definite that the men are going to buy clothes at The Bay, a chain of department stores in Canada. On being queried, she maintains her idea that the men are going shopping but offers an explanation inconsistent with her first one — that they are going to buy clothes. To do this, she assumes that something concrete was broken, which could be replaced at The Bay.

Episode 2

The net was hard to pull. The heavy sea and strong tide made it difficult even for the girdie. The meshed catch encouraged us to try harder.

STEVEN: It was not a very good day, as there were waves, which made it difficult for the girdie. That must be some kind of machine for doing something. The net could be for pulling something out of the water like an old wreck. No, wait! It said "meshed catch." I don't know why, but that makes me think of fish and, sure, if you caught

> fish, you'd really want to get them. [Any questions?] No
> questions, just that I think maybe the girdie is a machine
> for helping the men pull in the fish or whatever it was.
> Maybe a type of pulley.

COLLEEN: I guess The Bay must have a big water fountain. [Why
was the net hard to pull?] There's a lot of force on the
water. [Why was it important for them to pull the net?]
It was something they had to do. [What do you mean?]
They had to pull the net, and it was hard to do. [Any
questions?] No. [Where do you think they're going?]
Shopping.

For both children, the interpretations of Episode 2 build on those of
Episode 1. Steven continues to question what the men were doing. He
raises a number of alternative interpretations dealing with the context
of the sea. He refines his interpretations through testing hypothetical
interpretations against specific details, and hypotheses of specific word
meanings against his emerging interpretation of the story. At the outset, he
makes an inference that a girdie is a machine, but he leaves details about
its nature and function unspecified. He tentatively offers one specific use
for the net, but immediately questions this use when he realizes that it will
not account for the meshed catch, and substitutes an alternative function.
He then confirms this interpretation with the fact from the story that the
men were encouraged to try harder and his belief that if you catch fish,
you would really want to bring them aboard. Finally, he sees that he is in a
position to offer a more definitive but tentative interpretation of the word
"girdie."

Colleen maintains her interpretation of going shopping at The Bay.
When questioned about her interpretation, Colleen responds in vague
or tautological terms. She seems not to integrate information relating
to the terms "net," "catch," and "sea," and she seems satisfied to remain
uninformed about the nature of the girdie and the reason for pulling the
net. In the end, she concludes definitively that the men are going shopping.

Episode 3

With four quintels aboard, we were now ready to leave. The skipper saw mares' tails in the north.

STEVEN: I wonder what quintels are? I think maybe it's a sea term, a word that means perhaps the weight aboard. Yes, maybe it's how much fish they had aboard. [So you think it was fish?] I think fish or maybe something they had found in the water, but I think fish more because of the word "catch." [Why were they worried about the mares' tails?] I'm not sure. Mares' tails...let me see, mares are horses, but horses are not going to be in the water. The mares' tails are in the north. Here farmers watch the north for bad weather, so maybe the fishermen do the same thing. Yeah, I think that's it, it's a cloud formation, which could mean strong winds and hail or something I think could be dangerous if you were in a boat and had a lot of weight aboard. [Any questions?] No.

COLLEEN: They were finished with their shopping and were ready to go home. [What did they have aboard?] Quintels. [What are quintels?] I don't know. [Why were they worried about the mares' tails?] There were a group of horses on the street, and they were afraid they would attack the car. [Any questions?] No.

Steven is successful in his efforts to incorporate the new information into an evolving interpretation. From the outset, Steven acknowledges that he does not know the meaning of quintel and seeks a resolution of this unknown. He derives a meaning consistent with his evolving interpretation and with the textual evidence. In his attempt to understand the expression "mares' tails," he first acknowledges that he does not know the meaning of the expression. Thence, he establishes what he does know from the background knowledge (mares are horses, horses are not going to be in the water, there is nothing around except sky and water, farmers watch the north for bad weather) and textual information (the men are on the bay, they have things aboard, the mares' tails are in the north) and inferences he has previously made (the men are in a boat, they are fishing). He integrates this knowledge into a comparison between the concerns of Alberta farmers with which he is familiar, and what he takes to be analogous concerns of fishermen. On seeing the pertinence of this analogy, he draws the conclusion that the mares' tails must be a cloud formation foreboding inclement weather. He claims support for his conclusion in the fact that it would explain the skipper's concern for the mares' tails, indicating that he did not lose sight of the overall task of understanding the story.

Colleen maintains her original interpretation and does not incorporate all the new textual information into it. She works with the information on the men's leaving and the mares' tails but appears to ignore or remain vague about other information. For example, she says the cargo was comprised of quintels but indicates no effort to determine what these things are. She cites the fact that the men were ready to leave and suggests that they have finished their shopping, but does not attempt to explain the use of such words as "skipper", and "aboard" in the context of shopping for clothes. She interprets mares' tails as a group of horses that possibly would attack the men, but gives no account of what the horses might be doing on the street. Basically, she appears to grow tolerant of ambiguity and incompleteness in her interpretation.

In the episodes on the previous pages, notice how both readers illustrate the relationship between creative and critical thinking. Steve is creating an interpretation, actively constructing — building it, if you will — and, in so doing, he makes creative and constructive use of previous knowledge and of his imagination, critically assessing his interpretation as he goes. Colleen, by contrast, is certainly creative in one sense — wildly building a bizarre interpretation, unrestrained by mere reality or plausibility. (Later, after reading that the men cut up the fish they have caught, she, believing the fish to be guppies, says that after the men cut them up, they probably put them in an aquarium.) This creativity run amok is not true creative thought. Only a disciplined process of critical analysis enables one to create in one's mind the logic of the text, to construct a system of meanings that mirror, to the best of one's ability, the system of meanings inherent in the text.

Conclusion

Creativity, as a term of praise, involves more than a mere haphazard or uncritical making, more than the raw process of bringing something into being. It requires that what is brought into being meets criteria intrinsic to what it is we are trying to make. Novelty alone will not do, for worthless novelty is easy to produce. Intellectual standards and discipline, rightly used, do not stand in the way of creativity. Rather, they provide a way to begin to generate it — slowly and painfully, one problem at a time, one insight at a time.

If we learn to engage in genuine intellectual work on genuine intellectual problems worthy of reasoned thought and analysis, if we become a judicious critic of the nature and quality of our thought, we have done all we can do to become critically creative and creatively critical persons and thinkers. Stimulating intellectual work develops the intellect as both creator and evaluator: as a creator that evaluates and as an evaluator that creates. The result is fitness of mind, comprehensive intellectual excellence.

The Thinker's Guide Library

The Thinker's Guide series provides convenient, inexpensive, portable references that students and faculty can use to improve the quality of studying, learning, and teaching. Their modest cost enables instructors to require them of all students (in addition to a textbook). Their compactness enables students to keep them at hand whenever they are working in or out of class. Their succinctness serves as a continual reminder of the most basic principles of critical thinking.

For Students & Faculty

 Critical Thinking—The essence of critical thinking concepts and tools distilled into a 22-page pocket-size guide. **#520m**

 Analytic Thinking—This guide focuses on the intellectual skills that enable one to analyze anything one might think about — questions, problems, disciplines, subjects, etc. It provides the common denominator between all forms of analysis. **#595m**

 Asking Essential Questions—Introduces the art of asking essential questions. It is best used in conjunction with the Miniature Guide to Critical Thinking and the Thinker's Guide on How to Study and Learn. **#580m**

 How to Study & Learn—A variety of strategies—both simple and complex—for becoming not just a better student, but also a master student. **#530m**

 How to Read a Paragraph—This guide provides theory and activities necessary for deep comprehension. Imminently practical for students. **#525m**

 How to Write a Paragraph—Focuses on the art of substantive writing. How to say something worth saying about something worth saying something about. **#535m**

 The Human Mind—Designed to give the reader insight into the basic functions of the human mind and to how knowledge of these functions (and their interrelations) can enable one to use one's intellect and emotions more effectively. **#570m**

 Foundations of Ethical Reasoning—Provides insights into the nature of ethical reasoning, why it is so often flawed, and how to avoid those flaws. It lays out the function of ethics, its main impediments, and its social counterfeits. **#585m**

 How to Detect Media Bias and Propaganda—Designed to help readers recognize bias in their nation's news and come to recognize propaganda so they can reasonably determine what media messages need to be supplemented, counter-balanced or thrown out entirely. It focuses on the logic of the news as well as societal influences on the media. **#575m**

 Scientific Thinking—The essence of scientific thinking concepts and tools. It focuses on the intellectual skills inherent in the well-cultivated scientific thinker. **#590m**

 Fallacies: The Art of Mental Trickery and Manipulation—Introduces the concept of fallacies and details 44 foul ways to win an argument. **#533m**

For Students & Faculty, cont.

 Engineering Reasoning—Contains the essence of engineering reasoning concepts and tools. For faculty it provides a shared concept and vocabulary. For students it is a thinking supplement to any textbook for any engineering course. **#573m**

 Glossary of Critical Thinking Terms & Concepts—Offers a compendium of more than 170 critical thinking terms for faculty and students. **#534m**

 Aspiring Thinker's Guide to Critical Thinking—Introduces critical thinking using simplified language (and colorful visuals) for students. It also contains practical instructional strategies for fostering critical thinking. **#554m**

 Clinical Reasoning—Introduces the clinician or clinical student to the foundations of critical thinking (primarily focusing on the analysis and assessment of thought), and offers examples of their application to the field. **#564m**

 Critical and Creative Thinking—Focuses on the interrelationship between critical and creative thinking through the essential role of both in learning. **#565m**

 Intellectual Standards—Explores the criteria for assessing reasoning; illuminates the importance of meeting intellectual standards in every subject and discipline. **#593m**

For Faculty

 Active and Cooperative Learning—Provides 27 simple ideas for the improvement of instruction. It lays the foundation for the ideas found in the mini-guide *How to Improve Student Learning*. **#550m**

 Critical Thinking Competency Standards— Provides a framework for assessing students' critical thinking abilities. **#555m**

 Critical Thinking Reading and Writing Test—Assesses the ability of students to use reading and writing as tools for acquiring knowledge. Provides grading rubrics and outlines five levels of close reading and substantive writing. **#563m**

 Educational Fads— Analyzes and critiques educational trends and fads from a critical thinking perspective, providing the essential idea of each one, its proper educational use, and its likely misuse. **#583m**

 How to Improve Student Learning—Provides 30 practical ideas for the improvement of instruction based on critical thinking concepts and tools. **#560m**

 Socratic Questioning—Focuses on the mechanics of Socratic dialogue, on the conceptual tools that critical thinking brings to Socratic dialogue, and on the importance of questioning in cultivating the disciplined mind. **#553m**